THE SCIENCE BEHIND

Food

Casey Rand

Chicago, Illinois

www.capstonepub.com
Visit our website to find out more information about Heinemann-Raintree books.

To order:
☎ Phone 888-454-2279
🖥 Visit www.capstonepub.com to browse our catalog and order online.

Edited by Megan Cotugno and Laura Knowles
Designed by Richard Parker
Picture research by Mica Brancic
Original Illustrations © Capstone Global Library Ltd 2012
Illustrations by Oxford Designers & Illustrators

Originated by Capstone Global Library Ltd
Printed and bound in China by Leo Paper Products Ltd

15 14 13 12 11
10 9 8 7 6 5 4 3 2 1

Library of Congress Cataloging-in-Publication Data
Rand, Casey.
 Food / Casey Rand.
  p. cm.—(The science behind)
 Includes bibliographical references and index.
 ISBN 978-1-4109-4486-3 (hc)—ISBN 978-1-4109-4497-9 (pb) 1. Food—Juvenile literature. I. Title.
 TX355.R26 2012
 641.3—dc23   2011014586

Acknowledgments
We would like to thank the following for permission to reproduce photographs: Getty Images p. **9** (AFP Photo/Juan Mabromata); Shutterstock pp. **5** (© Stephen Coburn), **6** (© Laurent Dambies), **10** (© Vrvalerian), **13** (© MikeE), **14** (© Beth Van Trees), **15** (© Nayashkova Olga), **16** (© Peter Baxter), **18** (© Wavebreak Media ltd), **19** (© Eric Gevaert), **20** (© Michael C. Gray), **22** (© Suzanne Tucker), **24** (© Hfng), **25** (© YanLev), **21** bottom (© Arti_Zav), **21** top (© Atoss); USDA p. **8** (United States Department of Agriculture).

Cover photograph of a beautiful spread of fruits and vegetables reproduced with permission of Shutterstock/© Valentyn Volkov.

We would like to thank David Crowther and Nancy Harris for their invaluable help in the preparation of this book.

Every effort has been made to contact copyright holders of any material reproduced in this book. Any omissions will be rectified in subsequent printings if notice is given to the publisher.

Disclaimer
All the Internet addresses (URLs) given in this book were valid at the time of going to press. However, due to the dynamic nature of the Internet, some addresses may have changed, or sites may have changed or ceased to exist since publication. While the author and publisher regret any inconvenience this may cause readers, no responsibility for any such changes can be accepted by either the author or the publisher.

Contents

Look for these boxes:

Stay safe
These boxes tell you how to keep yourself and your friends safe from harm.

In your day
These boxes show you how science is a part of your daily life.

Measure up!
These boxes give you some fun facts and figures to think about.

Some words appear in bold, **like this**. You can find out what they mean by looking at the green bar at the bottom of the page or in the glossary.

Pizza is delicious! Have you ever wondered why pizza smells and tastes so good? Science has the answer. This book will teach you the science behind pizza, and lots of other foods, too!

Filling up

Your body can do lots of incredible things. These things cannot happen unless your body gets **nutrients**. Nutrients are what your body needs to function and grow. Your body gets many nutrients by eating food.

Carbohydrates:
Pizza crust is bread. Bread contains carbohydrates. Carbohydrates are a good **energy** source.

Vitamins and minerals:
Green peppers are vegetables. Fruits and vegetables have vitamins and minerals. They help us stay healthy.

The body needs five types of nutrients from food to function. Pizza has them all!

Fat:
Cheese comes from milk. Most milk products contain fat. Fat in our bodies stores extra energy.

Protein:
Pepperoni is a meat. Meat is a good source of protein. Protein helps build **muscles**.

energy source of usable power
muscle part of the body that you use to move

Eating food provides your body with **energy**. **Fats**, **proteins**, and **carbohydrates** contain this energy. Some foods provide your body with lots of energy. Some foods provide your body with less. When you are active, you use this energy.

Sun powered

The Sun is a giant ball of energy! Almost all of the energy on Earth comes from the Sun. Energy from the Sun is carried to Earth as light. Green plants have the ability to capture this energy. They change the Sun's energy into sugars. The process of changing the Sun's energy to sugar is known as **photosynthesis**.

The Sun's energy is captured by plants and gives energy for life on Earth.

Sun: The Sun sends energy to Earth.

Meat eaters: Some animals and humans get energy by eating other animals.

Plant eaters: Some animals and humans get energy by eating plants.

Plants: Energy from the Sun is taken in, changed into sugars, and stored.

carbohydrate main energy source used by the human body. Carbohydrates are produced by plants during photosynthesis.

photosynthesis process by which plants capture energy from light to make sugars

Delicious and Healthy

Food can be delicious and good to eat, but we also need food to live and to be healthy. The body needs many things found in food to survive and grow. Too much of some types of food and not enough of others can be very unhealthy.

MyPlate

The MyPlate food plate was created by doctors and scientists to help you make good food choices. You can use it to see if you are getting enough of the right foods in your diet. This plate can help you have a balanced diet.

The MyPlate food plate divides foods into four groups, with **dairy** on the side. Eating the right amounts will help your body stay healthy.

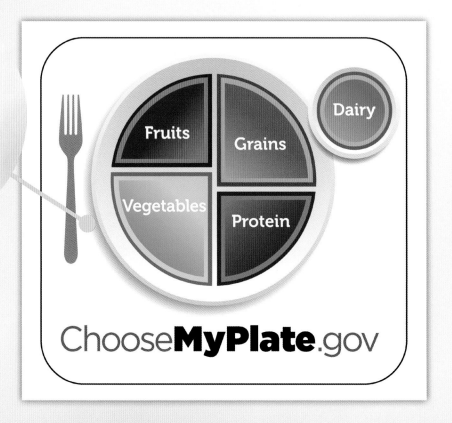

Athletes eat fruits and vegetables for **energy** and **nutrients**.

Measure up!

Make a note of the food you eat for a whole day. Use the MyPlate food plate to see if you are getting enough of each food group.

Grains

Many foods come from **grains** such as wheat, rice, and oats. Grains can be used to make bread, pasta, cereal, and lots of other foods. The MyPlate food plate tells us to eat lots of grains.

Farmers use huge machines to collect and store grains.

Carbohydrates

Foods made with grains are usually rich in **carbohydrates**. Carbohydrates are broken down into sugars by the body. These sugars give us **energy** for biking, climbing, and other activities. There are two major types of carbohydrates in food. They are complex carbohydrates and simple carbohydrates.

Complex carbohydrates

Most grain products are full of complex carbohydrates. These break down into sugar more slowly in your body. They keep you feeling full and energized longer.

Simple carbohydrates

Simple carbohydrates are also known as simple sugars. They break down quickly in the body. Sweet-tasting things such as chocolate and fruit usually contain simple carbohydrates. They give you a quick boost of energy, but it will not last long.

Fruits and Vegetables

Fruits and vegetables can help you stay fit and healthy. Fruits and vegetables are full of **vitamins and minerals**. Vitamins and minerals protect against disease and sickness.

Vitamins

Vitamins help the body to function. Your body cannot make its own vitamins and cannot store some types of vitamins. This means it is important to eat foods with lots of vitamins every day.

Stay safe

Vitamin D is very important for bone health. The body can make its own vitamin D when it is exposed to sunlight. However, you should always wear sunscreen when you are outside on a sunny day.

Eating fruits and vegetables will help you stay healthy.

Minerals

Just like vitamins, minerals help your body grow and function. Minerals are found mostly in the ground, but you do not have to eat soil to get them! Plants take in minerals from the ground for us. When you eat fruits and vegetables, you will get plenty of minerals.

Cheese, yogurt, and ice cream are delicious foods that are all made from milk. Products made from milk are called **dairy** products. Most dairy products are made from cow's milk, but milk from goats, buffalo, and sheep is also used.

Most dairy products are made from cow's milk. Dairy farmers today usually use machines to get milk from cows.

Cheese is made from milk. There are hundreds of kinds of cheese in the world.

Fats

Fat is found in most dairy products. Our body uses fat for growth, development, and to store extra **energy**. When more food is eaten than the body needs, the extra food is changed into fat and stored. This leads to weight gain, which can be unhealthy. For this reason, we should not eat too much fat.

In your day

While you are young, your body is making lots of new bone to help you grow! Your body needs to get lots of the mineral **calcium** for this. Dairy products are a great source of calcium.

calcium   mineral that helps keep bones and teeth strong and healthy

Meat and Beans

Do you want to work your **muscles**? Smile! There are 43 muscles just in your face, and smiling uses many of them. **Protein** helps build strong muscles. The meat and beans food group is full of foods rich in proteins. The group includes animal meats such as chicken, fish, and beef (from cows). Nuts, eggs, and beans are also part of this high-protein food group.

Fire up the grill

Sausages and hamburgers are delicious grilled. Grilling uses very high temperatures, and it is a popular way to cook meat. The heat comes from burning wood, coals, or gas.

Grilling is a great way to cook meat outdoors. But be careful around grills, as they are very hot!

The incredible egg

Eggs are one of the most amazing foods available. Eggs are easy to cook and do not cost a lot. They contain high-quality protein and many **vitamins and minerals**.

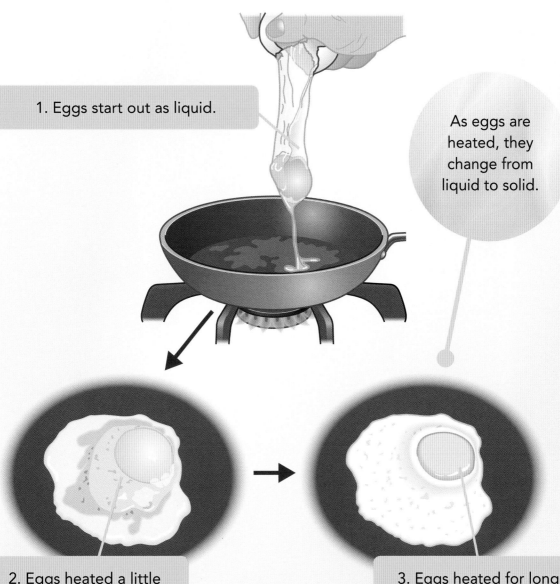

1. Eggs start out as liquid.

As eggs are heated, they change from liquid to solid.

2. Eggs heated a little are still soft.

3. Eggs heated for longer become firm.

In the Kitchen

A potato pulled from the garden is hard and dirty. We do not usually eat foods just as they are found in nature. We make changes to make them smell and taste better. Potatoes are cleaned, cut, and cooked to make them safe and delicious to eat.

The kitchen is full of tools and ingredients we can use to prepare food.

Tools of the kitchen

The kitchen is full of tools that we use to prepare food for eating.

- Blender: This is a kitchen tool with spinning blades that chop, cut, and mix.
- Rolling pin: This tool is shaped like a smooth log and used to roll dough.
- Refrigerator: This keeps food cold, so it stays fresh and safe to eat.

Make it hot

Adding or removing heat from food can change the way it looks and tastes. Cooking is the process of adding heat to food. It makes some foods smell and taste better. Removing heat from food, or making food cold, can help it taste better, too. Ice cream would not be so delicious if it were not frozen.

Cooking adds heat to food. It kills **germs** on some foods and makes them safer to eat.

Stay safe
Cooking should always be done with adult supervision. Sharp knives and hot stoves are dangerous.

germ tiny living thing that can cause illness

Smelling

One of the best things about cooking is the smell of food! When cookies are baked, many tiny parts of the cookie (too small to see) are released into the air. The human nose has a special patch inside it that senses these tiny parts. This is why you smell cookies when they are baking.

Your nose has a special patch used for sensing smell.

Tasting

Your mouth has thousands of tiny taste buds. They send messages to your brain about what you taste. But your sense of smell is also important to how foods taste. Scientists think that 75 percent of your sense of taste comes from what you smell!

Can you taste the difference? If you hold your nose, a bite of apple and onion will taste almost the same. Your sense of smell is very important to taste.

The five basic tastes

Taste buds can recognize five types of taste. They are sweet, salty, sour, bitter, and **umami** (a savory taste).

umami one of the five basic tastes. It is found in foods such as meats, cheeses, and vegetables.

Digestion

Your heart is not made of spinach. Your legs are not made of carrot sticks. So how does your body use the spinach and carrots you eat to help make your heart and legs work? **Digestion** is the answer. Digestion is the process your body uses to get **nutrients** and **energy** from food.

Bacteria? Yuck!

Bacteria are extremely tiny living things that live in and all around us. More than 500 types of bacteria live in your mouth! They sound horrible, but these bacteria are your friends. They protect you from less friendly bacteria that could make you sick.

Food begins to be digested as soon as it goes into your mouth!

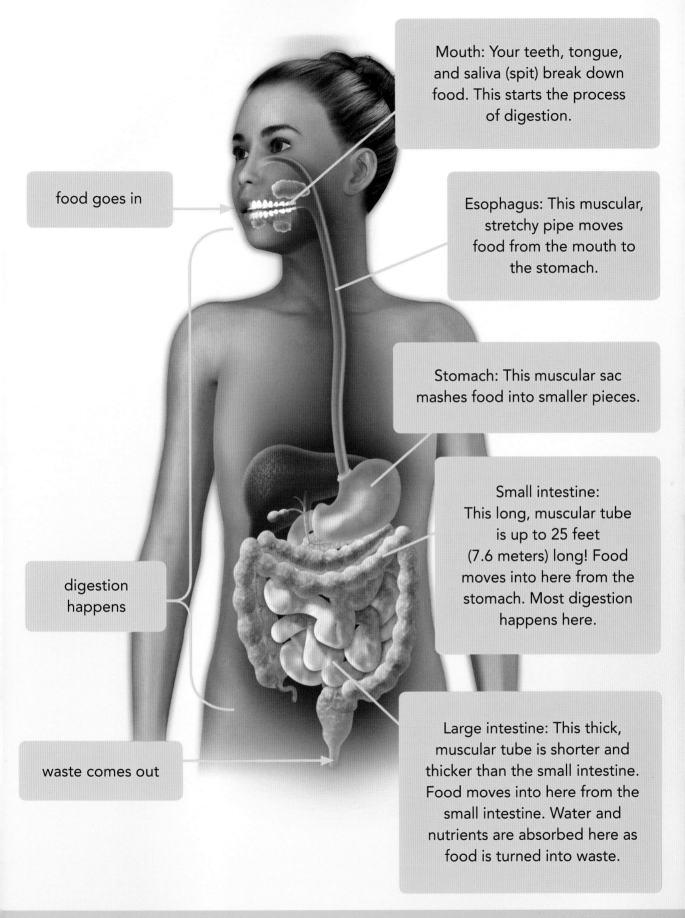

Mouth: Your teeth, tongue, and saliva (spit) break down food. This starts the process of digestion.

food goes in

Esophagus: This muscular, stretchy pipe moves food from the mouth to the stomach.

Stomach: This muscular sac mashes food into smaller pieces.

Small intestine: This long, muscular tube is up to 25 feet (7.6 meters) long! Food moves into here from the stomach. Most digestion happens here.

digestion happens

waste comes out

Large intestine: This thick, muscular tube is shorter and thicker than the small intestine. Food moves into here from the small intestine. Water and nutrients are absorbed here as food is turned into waste.

Solar-Powered You

Did you know you are **solar**-powered? Just like a solar-powered car, you convert **energy** from the Sun into movement and activity. You do not use the Sun's energy directly. First, plants change the Sun's energy into sugars through **photosynthesis**. When you eat plants, your body uses these sugars as fuel for your activities.

Like this solar-powered car, your body changes energy from the Sun into energy for movement.

Energy storage

Your body uses three major types of energy storage units. These are **fats**, **carbohydrates**, and **proteins**. Each stores energy and has special roles in your body. We need certain amounts of each. Using the MyPlate food plate can help you eat a balanced diet.

Making food work for you

Getting energy is not as easy as putting food into your mouth. We prepare and cook many foods to make them safe to eat and delicious. Once we start to eat, the process of **digestion** begins. Digestion breaks down food so we get the energy and **nutrients** we need.

Food gives us the energy we need to live, work, and play.

Try It Yourself

Make your own ice cream!

Now that you have learned all about the science behind food, try this fun and delicious experiment! Ask an adult to help you make this recipe.

What you need

- 2 tablespoons sugar
- ½ cup heavy cream and ½ cup milk, mixed together
- ½ teaspoon of vanilla extract
- ½ cup rock salt
- ice cubes (crushed works best)
- 2 tablespoons of nuts or crushed candy bar
- 1 medium zip-seal freezer bag
- 1 large zip-seal freezer bag

What to do

1. Combine the first three ingredients on the list in the smaller-size freezer bag and <u>seal it tightly</u>.

2. Place the salt and ice in the larger-size bag, then place the sealed smaller bag inside as well. Seal the larger bag.

3. Now gently shake the bags until the mixture in the small bag hardens (about 5 minutes).

4. Remove the smaller bag and add the nuts or crushed candy bar. Eat and enjoy!

You know that adding or removing heat from food can change how it looks and tastes. Before you start this experiment, try to guess how adding ice to your ingredients will make them change. Are you adding or removing heat? What do you think will happen?

Glossary

bacteria tiny living things that live in and all around us

calcium mineral that helps keep bones and teeth strong and healthy

carbohydrate main energy source used by the human body. Carbohydrates are produced by plants during photosynthesis.

dairy food made from milk

digestion process the body uses to break down food into small, usable parts

energy source of usable power

fat oily substance found in foods such as milk, cheese, and meat

germ tiny living thing that can cause illness

grain cereal grass, such as wheat

muscle part of the body that you use to move

nutrient source that provides the body with something it needs to function or grow

photosynthesis process by which plants capture energy from light to make sugars

protein nutrient important for building muscle and functioning in various roles in the body

solar to do with the Sun or sunlight

umami one of the five basic tastes. It is found in foods such as meats, cheeses, and vegetables.

vitamins and minerals substances important for normal growth and activity of the body and obtained naturally from plant and animal foods

Find Out More

Use these resources to find more fun and useful information about the science behind food.

Books

Bird, Fiona. *Kids' Kitchen: 40 Fun and Healthy Recipes to Make and Share*. Cambridge, Mass.: Barefoot Books, 2009.

Chancellor, Deborah. *Healthy Eating (Now We Know About...)*. New York: Crabtree, 2009.

O'Donnell , Liam. *The World of Food Chains with Max Axiom, Super Scientist (Graphic Science)*. North Mankato, Minn.: Capstone, 2008.

Royston, Angela. *Vitamins and Minerals for a Healthy Body (Body Needs)*. Chicago: Heinemann Library, 2009.

Thomas, Isabel. *Why Do I Burp? (Inside My Body)*. Chicago: Raintree, 2011.

Websites

kidshealth.org/kid/stay_healthy/food/vitamin.html
Find out more about the importance of vitamins and minerals for a healthy body on this KidsHealth website.

www.choosemyplate.gov
Visit this website to find out about the MyPlate food plate and how you can eat a balanced diet.

www.jamieoliver.com/us/foundation/jamies-food-revolution/school-food
Find out more about Jamie Oliver's campaign for better school cafeteria food.

www.smallstep.gov/kids/flash/index.html
Learn more about healthy eating at this website, which is full of fun activities and challenges.

Index